Nostalgic Waves from Soweto
Poetic Memories of the June 16th Uprising

Solrha

African Perspectives Publishing
PO Box 95342
Grant Park 2051
South Africa
Email: francis@africanperspectives.co.za
www.africanperspectives.co.za

© Solhra 2009

ISBN 978-0-9814398-0-8

Edited by Mindy Stanford
Typeset by Gail Day
Cover design by Mycalture
Printed and bound by 4 Colour Print

Contents

About Sol Rachilo

Sol "Solrha" Rachilo was a child of the turbulence and upheaval of Soweto as the struggle for freedom grew in the hearts and minds of the young.

Wanting to make a meaningful contribution, like so many of his generation, Sol completed social work studies at the Jan Hofmeyer Institute and almost by accident, stumbled on the world of theatre and writing.

The late Ken Gampu, a close friend who later became South Africa's first internationally recognised actor, invited him to auditions that an unspecified white man from the University of Cape Town was holding for an unnamed play. The play in question was "No Good Friday" and the white man was Athol Fugard, who was carving out the first steps in his own climb to international fame.

Sol admits that at first, he didn't take the theatre seriously. It was Fugard who opened his eyes to the importance of theatre in reflecting life, which made him realise that through theatre and writing he could develop and project his own complex personality and identity. His growing commitment to this fascinating world resulted in his selection for the lead in Fugard's "Nongogo".

Already a voracious reader, thanks to the mentorship and nurture of a Scottish doctor who practically adopted him during his first ten years, Sol was soon burning with ideas that needed expression. The young Sol's passion was fuelled by the ready access he had to literature through his father's bookshop in White City, Jabavu. Moses China Rachilo had founded the bookstore in a determined drive to provide books for schools in the vicinity. The shop was soon discovered by people who were hungry for intellectual stimulus, and among the frequent callers was Nadine Gordimer, still a fast friend.

By 1967 Sol had written his first musical, "Three in Number". Set to music by Gideon Nxumalo with musicians of the stature of Dennis Nene and Morris Manana, it was a milestone in Sol's own emotional and artistic flowering. The plays that were to follow would lead him to poetry, where he developed new dimensions of expression.

Strongly driven by a concern for young people, by 1977 Sol had founded the Cosac Drama Academy. Here, future actors for the television industry and other realms of creativity have been groomed and moulded. Among the academy's graduates are Themba Khumalo, news editor of the *Daily Sun;* Nandi Nyembe of "Zone 14" and "Zola 7"; Lotto presenter, Nimrod Nkosi; and Kenneth Nkosi of "Tsotsi".

Today, in addition to continuing the Cosac Academy, Sol manages a production company called Inner Eye Production and Artists' Management.

Foreword

In *Nostalgic Waves from Soweto*, we see, feel, hear, touch and smell the human debris made by a cruel time as the poet's scalpel cuts, leaving mysterious thin red lines, which drip to open and reveal the worst of human deeds and experience. These revelations, embedded in the hearts, minds and acts of men and women, are caught in a long moment of time, which lingers in these poems, where every line asks: why do humans do these things?

As a veteran cultural worker, Bra Sol whispers all kinds of things to us. He knows the apartheid system has been crushed by sheer human will power and sacrifice, he knows that we have called for reconciliation; that we have told the world that we want to forgive; that we are taking steps to move away from that past to a future which we build with vision and skill. Bra Sol knows all these things, but still, he asks: do we want to forget? And his answer is a resolute No – these things must not be forgotten, they cannot be forgotten, they are not to be forgotten, and we will only incubate peril if we forget them.

Bra Sol has walked the streets of Soweto, Alexandra, Mamelodi, Kwa Mashu, Athlone, Berea; he has also been to Yeoville, Bishops Court, Houghton, even as he stretches his mind, he has walked

> to the decks of the heaving ships
> crossing from continent to continent
> their bellies full of men and goods...

In these poems where the worst of life is laid bare, the human spirit forever reveals itself as a miracle and a mystery of human love.

Mongane W Serote
October 2009

Introduction

Soweto during the 1970s was riven with violence and brutality,
the brunt of which was borne by the young people of that
period, who took the lead in the struggle against apartheid
oppression. Himself a product of the era, Sol Rachilo turned
both to science and to art as he strove to depict the atmosphere
and the emotions of the people of those tumultuous times
through the prose poetry of "Nostalgic Waves from Soweto".

Not relying solely on his own deeply engraved memories,
he spent 18 months researching the events which swirled around
the Morris Isaacson High School, a magnet for the activists and
intellectuals of the time. The book especially highlights the
happenings of 1976 and 1977, two years of strife in this
politically charged township which was the home of all the
founding fathers of what Sol calls, "our cherished freedom" –
Nelson Mandela, Walter Sisulu, Nthato Motlana, Desmond Tutu,
Mothopeng and Sobukwe.

Drawing on the wide-ranging artistic experience gained in
his years of acting and writing for theatre, Sol first ventured
into poetry in 1977. Here he found he could more intensely
express the thoughts and feelings garnered from his acute sense
of observation. People, their interaction with the environment
and the socio-political and cultural times, the pains and hopes
of a generation and the multi-facetted world of an evolving
Johannesburg are the inspiration of his deeply-felt poems and
ballads.

Ordinary activities, every-day occurrences, a chance
conversation overheard between two street-cleaners, the brutal
death of a young political activist at the hands of security
police, observations on the crime, violence and morals of
naked Soweto – all are evoked in haunting, nostalgic and
sometimes ironic reminiscences which recreate a period slowly
fading from memory.

He turns a blistering spotlight on some incidents,
encapsulated in a few, searing words. Others he treats with
tenderness, understanding and an empathy which resounds
within the reader's own emotions. Life at its most basic is
counterbalanced by deep philosophic probings. There are

unspoken challenges for us to question and act as did the young people of those chaotic '70s.

These prose poems reflect a determination of Sol's to help bridge the gap which he believes is widening between the pre- and post-freedom generations. He feels intensely the importance of the artist's role in depicting the emotional and cultural evolution taking place in Johannesburg, which he views as the heart and essence of music, theatre, writing and artistic creativity. The poems mirror his own profound awareness of life, its variegated richness and its unlimited potential.

Nostalgic Waves from Soweto

Poetic Memories of the June 16th Uprising

'X'

I have gone to funerals
To show my last respects
To the dearly beloved ones.
At the graveside
I have witnessed scrolls,
Epitaphs, and heroes
Immortalized in ink.
But the bedrock of the struggle,
The fundament of the liberation movement,
Is forged from the uncountables:
Those insignificant names
The ones that were committed to the hilt
The unknown soldiers of the struggle
Who signed with a simple fingerprint
Or with an X.
Those who had no family left
To mourn their passing
Nothing written on their graves.

And if someone happens to remember
And comes searching for X
Or the grave of X,
An acquaintance may softly say:
"He's buried somewhere in Mshenguville."

The Signatories

If they had a mouth to speak
These eavesdropping corridors
Would share untold secrets
From the lips statesmen:
The ones who stood aloof,
Pen in hand, averting their gaze
As they signed into being
The untold misery.
As they signed away livelihoods
And lives

Boots in the Night

In the depth of night
When we are sojourning
With our spiritual gods,
Rapping thunder at the door…
Toe jong! Toe jong!
Bang! Crash!
The bin that stands against the door
Clatters and spews its garbage
Boots stomping and kicking,
Boots levelled at sleeping heads
Question questions
Rifling through our lives
Snatching our literature
Stealing our poems
Leaving us to pick up the trash
And once again to commune
With the gods of night

Lament
June 16, 1976

It was a regular day
Casting warmth on all humans.
The sun rose from the East
And later, in its glowing amber
It would set in the West.
But as it were,
History had marked the day
As the turning point
In the lives of these humans.
It was to a dual
Of "young guns" without guns
Pitted against the weight of the incumbent
The tanks and rifles of oppression.

Shouts, screams and blasts echoed
Through the dusty Soweto streets
Acrid fumes of teargas merged with gunpowder,
Choking the throats of wide-eyed children
As they braved bullets and baton blows
Their fresh blood reddening the streets
Their young bodies littering the unpaved kerbs
Over which the heavy "hippos"
Cast their evil shadows

* *guns: tsotsi talk for youthful gangs or "young guns"*
* *hippos: armoured military vehicles*

Child Crushed by Casspir

It's helter-skelter
Gunshots, sirens from police vans
Youth engulfed in teargas
No streetlights.
The youth up in arms
Pitted against the powers that be,
Rightless, and at the mercy
Of a ruthless regime.

No lights in the streets,
Only the glare of a helicopter searchlight
As it scans the dark streets,
Zooms in on a stationary Casspir,
And there:
Next to the heavily treaded wheel,
Ragged and mutilated,
The crushed body of child.

In the dark all around,
Afraid for their lives
Jabavu's youth whistle and groan
As the helicopter,
A stuttering predator,
Descends to the street
To claim another body
For the coldness of the mortuary slab

One of the Next Seven

Untimely though it is
The time for Xuma to leave
Has arrived.
His fiancée, is highly expectant
But he must go:
The mine has taken seven lives,
Replacements have been ordered.
He gazes at his ailing mother
On the eve of his departure,
And at the naked breast
And rounding belly
Of his wife to be.
Will it be a boy?
Will he be among the next seven?

The Creation of an Innocent Criminal

Loyal to the struggle
Always paid his dues promptly
Never missed a single meeting
Always optimistic
Never faltering
In anything he did
And when they raised their hands
With fists clenched
And hollered: "MAYIBUYE!"
He was always there to respond
"IZOBUYA!"

So it was that a peace loving man
Found himself on the run
But not for reasons he might have expected
He was simply paying a visit
To an ailing relative
A relative who happened to reside
In the servant zone
Of a Pretoria suburb
Where at night his human presence
Had been declared illegal

Two uniformed pistols pointing at him
His reaction instantaneous
Acknowledgement of Jha
Plus a jungle knife
Cleared him out of that fracas
Leaving the two white nationals
Breathing their last
And him forever
On the run

Eleventh Hour

In trying to turn the tide
He had gone to extremes
Applied unusual measures
Unethical measures
Now at this eleventh hour
All efforts to gain back his freedom
Had evaporated like a chimera
And the dreaded hour had come
The irrevocable date with the hangman

As the clock's pendulum
Swung from side to side
Echoing the beat of his heart
He felt again his child self:
The good and lovable altar boy
Who had wanted to follow
In the footsteps of his priestly father

The Black Cloth

for Mrs Makhubu who passed away in 2008

Is it forever,
until your son returns from exile?
The tattered seams of your black dress
Have been replaced again and again
Three decades and more
Your heart laden with sorrow
And the avoidable black cloth
Unzima lomthwalo

Comrade Chris

for Chris Hani, assassinated 10th April, 1993

Your passing, to many of us
Remains fresh and raw.
A fight well fought
You came back home
Ready to face the next battle
Unafraid to speak your heart
Ready to hear the voice
Of people on the ground.
And our ancestors
Thinking much had been won
In the return of their son
Dropped their guard
Just long enough
For the dark shadows
Waiting in the wings
To take their aim

Nomzamo

Mother of the nation
Banished and branded
Torn from your family
Alone, yet resolute
You were chosen
To step onto the
Rickety ladder of fame
And with your deeds
To make it firm
Long live Nomzamo!
Long live!

To Stompie

The newborn arrival's mother
Decided to console herself
By calling him
STOMPIE

Her choice was well received
The child grew
With all the grinding factors
That any township boy yields to

A break to see the bright lights of Jozi
Found Stompie in the company of Mandela
Part of a controversial soccer team
Stompie edged his way

The long, exciting nocturnal escapades
Punctuated by unending jokes in the garage
Always left part of the group
An emotional and physical wreck

A sad note, though,
Left a ... situation

Soweto, I Salute You

Your courage
Your resilience
For having cast in our midst
Leadership qualities of repute –
In Tata Sisulu
Tata Madiba
Tata Vundla
Tata Sobukwe
Tata mpilo Tutu
Ntate Motlana
All those who hailed from this ghetto
And led the battle
Gunless from within
Alongside the youth,
Who carried the cross
In their own way

And alongside those in exile
Who battled from without:
Soweto
I salute you!

Melody for a Father

He sat down
Pen in hand
Pondering ideas
For a new creation

Then it came to him
Like a wind that you feel
But cannot touch:
"A melody for my father
The person who sired my birth."

Then he felt the wind
And the cold absence:
"Granny never spoke about him
Mother never told me his names
He is a wind that blows
And comes then goes
Then comes again and goes."
And the song kept burning in him
And the wind came
And the wind went

Longing to Be Loved

There is an emptiness in my heart
An insatiable thirst
A thirst for love
And to be loved
Too long I've kept myself to myself
It's time for me to open this lonely heart
And let Cupid's arrow find its mark

The Couple's Song

The song had ended
And the singer had left the stage
But the melody lingered on.
It was pure nostalgia for the two
As they sat around the small table
Reflecting how they had begun together:
They recalled the scorn of their peers
The jibes about their platonic bond
The foundation of their early attraction.
They relived that first date:
Same place, same time
The bliss of the singer's melody
The pure passion of the lyrics
The thunderous applause
Then the gunshot behind the scenes
And the horror in the patrons' faces,
How together they had taken flight into the night.
Now again seated round the small table
The song had ended
And they felt it to be theirs

As Luck Would Have It

It was pouring heavily
Lightning streaking across the sky.
I stood there unable to cross
Because of the heavy flood.
A car was coming towards me
Flashing its lights.
The driver stopped,
Removed an obstruction from the road.

Then, out of the misty blue
Three human figures emerged.
They cornered him,
Held him to ransom.
A wad of notes extracted
An exchange of words
A sharp slap
A knife blade, two revolvers
A single shot hit its mark
With an uncharacteristic twang.
The man staggered towards his car
Slumped in the mud
Then, bleeding, looked up at me
And said: pointing at his skull
With an incongruous grin:
"That's number two,
The last bullet hole
Is right here
Under this steel plate.
This time I was lucky,
You could say it was a bull's eye!"

Uskhova Wasemasotsheni eB.E.S.L.
(British Empire Service League)

Day in and day out
Sitting on his rocking chair
Under a battered panama hat
uSKHOVA
The World War Two soldier
Who fought with the allies in Egypt
Now a recluse, old and infirm
Passing his days
At the British Empire Service League
in Dube
Suddenly, he leaps to attention:
Gives a full and rigid salute to his army seniors
As an aircraft drones across his horizon

His contemporaries long gone
Day in and day out
uSKHOVA sits in his rocking chair
Puffing his almost finished cigar
Admiring a youthful beauty passing by.
The next woman to pass
Keeping the sun off with an umbrella
Is old and loose fleshed
Counting her summers before passing on.
uSKHOVA's eyes are glued on her
Rocking in his chair he chants:
"Must be jelly 'cause jam don't shake lak dat...
Must be jelly 'cause jam don't shake lak dat..."

In two shakes of a duck's tail
The scene changes
And the last we see of SKHOVA
Is his torn Panama hat
Lying beside the rocking chair
Still rocking its lonesome rhythm
And the sharp point of an umbrella
Stuck on the corner of the window
UZO WUZ'UMOYA!

Profession of Despair

It's not a case of mistaken identity
She has joined the club
The ladies of the night.
Too long she kept faith
Loved loyally, served blindly
Washing his soiled clothes
Feeding his hungry mouth

She wanted little
Other than his loyalty
Other than his heart
"Till death do us part"

It was the letter
Hidden in a pocket:
"The maintenance is late
Our children need books, uniforms…"
She spread open the page
Laid it neatly on his jacket

Then took to the streets
To join her many sisters of despair
"Till death do us part"

Night Sweepers

The night talk is never dull
As they clean away
The dirt of the day
"Ma-Nkele had a
secret abortion
And who was the illicit lover?
None other than the priest!"

"Shosholoza" they cry
To give themselves steam
To keep the streets clean
"Zuma's pride
A fourth wife
Added to the collection"
"Shosholoza!"
The night is never dull
A burst of laughter
"Do you remember
At the corner of Ngema Street
The scavenger caught with his pants down
In Mam Tshawe's bedroom?
The only way out,
The broken ceiling
Leaving behind two exhibits:
A dompas and soiled underwear
Uyalayeka!"
(serves him right)
"Shosholoza!"
The night has a thousand eyes

What Lurks

What lurks?
In the mind of the robber
The rapist
The hijacker
Under the white-collar of the executive
What lurks in the mind of the city slicker
Of the taxi driver
The syndicate member
What is it that lurks there?
And also here?

Oliver Twist in Soweto

The social fabric is being rent in twain
To produce a recurring social threat
The next port of call
Is fertile and accommodating Hillbrow
Where derelict buildings offer better refuge

Through broken marriages
Fathers denying paternity
Mothers refuting maternity
They are here to stay

They are "asking for more"
At your corner shop
"Madam, can I carry your groceries?"

Small offenders,
Trivial transgressions
Innocent children
With no comprehension
That on this day
Under the shining sun
They are taking the first small step
On a long and hopeless road
That leads to delinquency

Baby Found in Plastic Bag

This ignominious deed
Could happen nowhere else
Except in umZansi
The profligate spender of human life
Where ubuntu,
Wrapped in a toilet roll
Has been cast down the drain
Where shame has sunken
Beneath the depths of depravity
Can a miracle emerge?
And curb our sick society
From this inhuman behaviour
So that once again umZansi
Can gain respect from the world at large
So we no longer need to hear ourselves called
The Rape Capital

The Night She Passed On

Murder most foul!
Yelled the man of the law
On finding the body of a female
Tangled in torn sheets
Spattered all over with blood
Motionless she lay
Alongside the gifts
The food parcels
She would never give
To her waiting siblings

Something to Live for

She had been unfortunate
The sangoma uncovered a curse
In the Dlamini family
That ran through its entire lineage

How can the Dlamini family
Be an exception to the ruling
That the preacher hollered on Sunday;
"You shall reap not what you sow
But also what your fathers sowed."

She pondered her plight:
Why me?
All the other young girls
Are fruitful and conceiving
At the tender age of 14!
I would also like
To behold my miracle;
A baby!

With her last five bob
S'true's bob
She put it on the sangoma's mat
He looked into his dolosse bones
And exclaimed:
Haikona, my child
I will not lie to you
The future is bleak
And I see nothing
"Take your five bob back."

In utter desperation
She languished around
Mam Tshwane's
In Dlamini too,
Just for the kick of it

Matshidiso

for Matshidiso Mashinini

From the cradle
She watched over them:
Those infant heads
In tattered shacks
Of uncertain shelter.
From the cradle she
Watched their smiles and tears
And wondered at the miracle:
How some of our little siblings
Reared in cesspools of disease and dirt
Exposed to hail and wind and rain
Have found a place in the sun

The Cripple at the Party

SEKUNJALO!
SES'KHONA!
That was the message
In the music
Upbeat!
Take it or leave it!
Girls swaying
Gyrating their bums
That tickled one's fancy

Coming towards the crippled man
An ecstatic one yelled:
"Come on baby,
Join me on a magic carpet ride
Feel the clouds up there
This ganja weed
Is causing waves
Come rock with my heart for sure."

He answered:
"I am rocking with mine."
Dancing closer,
He caught sight of her
As she made a u-turn.
He tried to reach out to her
But landed on the cold floor.

She turned, just to gaze
At him on the floor
Picking him up and cuddling him
She reassured:
"Forget the music
I'll dance with you in my heart."

What Change is There?

The freedom that rang from far
Is now at the doorstep
But what of it?
I peep through this window
And gaze at a white child
Chaperoned by its mother
To the school gate
Where is the black mother
Who can do the same in the ghetto?
She is forever hurrying, forever late
Scrambling to reach Mrs Slovo's kitchen
In Illovo
Rushing to get the vacuuming done
What change is there?

Loose Cannons

Black kids have become loose cannons
Girls fall pregnant
Give birth in toilets in the veld
Their babies dumped
Mourned by birds and flies
While discos overflow 'till dawn
It's a race for earthly pleasures
That beclouds the minds of youth

My Soweto Dream

What happens to a dream deferred?
Does it dry up
Like a cocoon
When the moth has hatched?
Or fester like a sore
And then run?
Does it stink like rotten meat
Or crust over like damp sugar?
Maybe it just sags
Like a heavy load
Or does it explode?

Silent Words

Words spoken in whispers
Cut as sharp as Shaka's spear
Words trapped at the tip of the tongue
Hold back hideous secrets
While a mother's broken silence
Falls on deaf ears

Looking Through the Hazy Glass

As I look through the hazy glass
Life has lost its colour
Everything in black or white
And inside: a deep dark hollow
A shadow that cannot move away
An emptiness that nothing seems to fill
In the gloom of this winter afternoon

The Grave

My empty grave awaits me
But reserve that rectangular hollow
For the countless numbers
Who lie abandoned at the city morgue
Heaped up and unclaimed
No earthly relatives

Or spare it for the lost ones
The young hijackers meeting
An untimely death
'In the line of duty'
Or for the two young bodies
Left to lie motionless
In the filthy waters of Mofolo stream

These bodies: let *them* lie
In the grave reserved for me
(In any case,
I'm planning to bunk the untimely call
As I've opted for cremation)

The Tree By the River

Down by the river
There is a tree
An unusual tree
The strange thing about this tree
Is that its human visitors
Always there for a rendezvous
Never clash
Not an ugly word is ever said
And always, they come in pairs
No matter what time of day or night
What is its magic?
I've never known
But all I wish
Is that all evil doers
Those without love in the heart
Just for one night
Pay this tree a courtesy call

The Torch

In my hand I have a torch
Before I pass it on
To direct another generation
Let me ignite it
Like the burning spear of liberation
Let me liberate myself
From the captivity of my mind
From inner hate syndrome
From the slave mentality of my youth
Stones, guns, spears and words
Hope and fear, tears of sorrow
All united for a single cause

Caged in Your Mind

Better to be a loose cannon
Than trapped in the labyrinth
Of a tormented mind
Better to be a misguided scud missile
Than to be spellbound in Hell

Awake but Not Alone

Morning comes and night falls
And on my pillow I lie
Awake, but not alone
I have travelled down this road
United and empowered by the Almighty
The one whom some call Jah

Dreaming of the Future

It is imperative to encourage innovation
Because change is in our lifeblood
Stagnation is our death knell
And the future lies in the mind

Paradise

The Holy Scriptures herald
A place of unrivalled grandeur
A reservoir of scenic beauty

If anyone attains perfection
One's company could be graced
By angelic souls
Radiating silvery white
Like doves floating on air
Geared like guided scud missiles
To wonderful destinations

So how could this rhapsodic splendour
Be brought to an abrupt ending
For the loving twosome
Naked Adam, naked Eve?

Could it be hope
On this armchair exploration
Is it hope deferred
Which makes the heart sick?

Remember

Let those who live
Remember the bad
For it can be improved upon
While the good remains always
Unchanged in the heart of man

But Once

I shall pass this way but once
So any good that I can do
Let me not defer
And any kindness I can show
To any human being
Let me not neglect
For I shall not pass
This way again

Miracles Abound

I know of nothing but miracles
Whether I walk the streets of Soweto
Or cast my eye over the reefs of makeshift dwellings
Below the Mshenguville skyline
Every cubic inch of Earth's extent is a miracle
Whether I wade barefoot along the Mofolo stream
Or stand under the gracious trees of a city park
Whether I chat by day with those I love
Or share a meal at the dinner table
Every hour of light and dark is a miracle
What stranger miracles can there be
Than the sea's unceasing swing from pole to pole
Its waters shimmering with fishes,
Than the heaving ships crossing from continent to continent
Their bellies full of men and goods?
I know of nothing but miracles